0702933

W9-ASE-798

0 1021 0218337 7

ON LINE

JBIOG
Roddi
Wheeler, Jill C.

Andy Roddick /

AWESOME ATHLETES

ANDY RODDICK

Jill C. Wheeler

ABDO Publishing Company

visit us at
www.abdopublishing.com

Published by ABDO Publishing Company, 4940 Viking Drive, Edina, Minnesota 55435.
Copyright © 2007 by Abdo Consulting Group, Inc. International copyrights reserved in all
countries. No part of this book may be reproduced in any form without written permission from
the publisher. The Checkerboard Library™ is a trademark and logo of ABDO Publishing
Company.

Printed in the United States.

Cover Photo: Getty Images
Interior Photos: AP/Wide World pp. 4, 5, 19, 21, 25; Corbis pp. 6, 7, 9, 14, 15, 18, 28-29; Getty
    Images pp. 13, 15, 17, 22, 24, 27; Peter Read Miller/Sports Illustrated p. 20;
    Ron C. Angle/Sports Illustrated p. 23; Sports Chrome p. 11

Series Coordinator: Rochelle Baltzer
Editors: Rochelle Baltzer, Heidi M. Dahmes
Art Direction: Neil Klinepier

Library of Congress Cataloging-in-Publication Data

Wheeler, Jill C., 1964-
   Andy Roddick / Jill C. Wheeler.
      p. cm. -- (Awesome athletes)
   Includes index.
   ISBN-10 1-59928-307-7
   ISBN-13 978-1-59928-307-4
   1. Roddick, Andy, 1982---Juvenile literature. 2. Tennis players--United States--Biography--
Juvenile literature. I. Title. II. Series.

   GV994.R63W44 2007
   796.342092--dc22
                                                                              2005036259

Contents

Andy Roddick 4

Athletic Family 6

On to Florida 8

Getting Game 10

Junior Champion 12

The Making of an Awesome Athlete 14

Turning Pro 16

U.S. Open Champion 20

On Tour 22

Roddick Today 26

Glossary 30

Web Sites 31

Index 32

Andy Roddick

Many people have tagged Andy Roddick as the rising star of American tennis. He has the most powerful serve on the **Association for Tennis Professionals (ATP)**

Tour. His **forehand** is fierce. Yet perhaps most important, Roddick is **passionate** about the game.

"Andy plays with enthusiasm," said Patrick McEnroe, one of Roddick's coaches. "He gets excited, he gets into it, he gets ticked off. People want to see the kind of passion he brings to the game."

Roddick gets fired up during a heated match!

Sometimes, Roddick's focus on the game is incredible. His temper is not as apparent as that of former tennis star John McEnroe. However, Roddick's emotions do surface at times. He broke 39 tennis rackets in 2002 alone!

Roddick does not fall into the typical tennis player role. His **charisma** has made him popular both on and off the court. Roddick retains his charming, easy-going personality on talk shows and at celebrity events.

Roddick's powerful serve and focus set him apart from other tennis players.

Athletic Family

Andrew Stephen Roddick was born on August 30, 1982, in Omaha, Nebraska. Andy's father, Jerry, was a businessman. His mother, Blanche, worked as a teacher before becoming a homemaker. Andy has two older brothers, Lawrence and John.

The Roddick family has always been interested in sports. Blanche especially enjoyed tennis and encouraged her sons to play the game. Playing tennis eventually became a family tradition, even on Christmas Eve! John quickly blossomed into the family's first tennis star.

In 1987, the Roddicks moved from Omaha to Austin, Texas. Austin would be a better place for John to advance his tennis career. Soon after the move, young Andy began playing tennis. He recalls playing imaginary games against the garage door. Andy pretended to compete against tennis greats Ivan Lendl and Boris Becker.

At 22, German tennis player Boris Becker won the 1989 U.S. Open.

Andy became more involved in tennis when he was about eight years old. He started taking group lessons and competing in local amateur tournaments.

Blanche recalls Andy showed good sportsmanship at a young age. One time during a **doubles** tournament, he noticed a boy without a partner. Andy recognized that he had talent. So Andy offered to partner with him, and they became friends.

For Andy's ninth birthday gift, his parents took him to the U.S. Open. The tournament was held in Flushing Meadows-Corona Park, New York.

On to Florida

In 1993, the Roddicks moved from Austin to Boca Raton, Florida. Once again, the family relocated so that John could further his tennis career. Florida is home to many tennis schools and professional players. This made it easier for John to focus on his game.

Andy took advantage of John's tennis connections. During one of his brother's tournaments, ten-year-old Andy met an official from Reebok. "My name is Andy," he told the official. "I'm going to be a great tennis player, and this is your chance." His sales pitch worked! Reebok invited Andy to join its junior tennis program.

Now, Andy had his work cut out for him. He was small for his age, so he focused on his strengths to win matches. Soon, he learned to use his serving abilities and speed to his advantage.

Meanwhile, John went on to become a tennis star at the University of Georgia. However, a back injury cut his tennis career short. Later, John started a tennis academy in San Antonio, Texas.

Andy developed his tennis skills in Boca Raton. Later, he bought his own home there.

Getting Game

Andy continued to work on his game. He began to advance in the junior rankings. When he was 14, he was invited to attend a tennis academy in Tampa, Florida. He tried it, but he returned home within weeks. Andy really enjoyed tennis. Yet he wanted to experience other things, too.

So, Andy attended Boca Preparatory International School. He was a good student, and he enjoyed playing basketball on the school's team. Outside of school, tennis kept him busy. Every day, Andy worked on his game with French coach Tarik Benhabiles.

In 1997, Andy realized that the traditional serving motion was not for him. So, he developed his own method. This way, he could serve faster and harder. When Andy was just 17 years old, his serve was clocked at 125 miles per hour (201 km/hr)!

Opposite Page: Andy's greatest strength has always been his power. So, he has had to work to improve his "mental" game. Andy believes tennis is more of a mental than physical game for professional players.

Junior Champion

In 1999, Andy trained with high school basketball teammate and fellow junior tennis player Mardy Fish. Fish moved in with the Roddicks to train with Andy and Benhabiles.

The two players began their days at 6:30 AM with 90-minute practices. At 2:00 PM, they hit the court again for another four hours of practice.

The **intense** training paid off soon enough. Andy won junior tournaments while still in high school. In December 1999, he titled at the Eddie Herr International Junior Tournament. This event attracts the top junior prospects from all over the world.

In January 2000, Andy earned a junior boys' title at the Australian Open. This was the first time an American had achieved this honor since 1959!

The Australian Open is one of four Grand Slam competitions in professional tennis. The other three are the French Open, Wimbledon, and the U.S. Open. If a player wins all four events, it is called a grand slam.

Andy and Mardy continued to play tennis together after high school. In 2004, they both took part in the Summer Olympics in Athens, Greece.

THE MAKING OF AN AWESOME ATHLETE

Andy Roddick is one of America's emerging tennis stars. His outstanding talent and sparkling personality bring excitement to the court.

1982	1993	1999	2000
Born on August 30, in Omaha, Nebraska	Joins Reebok junior tennis program	Titles at Eddie Herr International Junior Tournament	Becomes first American since 1959 to win a junior title at the Australian Open

How Awesome Is He?

Roddick has the most powerful serve on the ATP Tour. In September 2004, he set a new world record for serving. The ball was clocked at 155 miles per hour (250 km/h)! Roddick was ranked number one for serve speed at the 2005 U.S. Open.

Player	Serve Speed (mph)
Andy Roddick	**150**
Taylor Dent	148
Ivo Karlovic	142
Mark Philippoussis	141

ANDY RODDICK

**ATP TOURNAMENT WINS: 20 SINGLES,
    2 DOUBLES**
PLAYS: RIGHT-HANDED
HEIGHT: 6 FEET, 2 INCHES
WEIGHT: 190 POUNDS

2001	2002	2003	2004
Wins first tournament as a professional	Becomes youngest American to finish in year-end ATP Top Ten since 1992	Wins U.S. Open	Leads United States to first Davis Cup final since 1997

- Finished 2005 in the ATP top three worldwide for the third straight year and as the number one American ATP player

- Represented the United States at the 2004 Summer Olympics in Athens, Greece

- Key player on the U.S. Davis Cup team since 2001

Highlights

Turning Pro

As his high school days drew to a close, Andy had to make an important decision. He could attend college on a tennis **scholarship** as his brother John had done. Or, he could become a tennis professional. Andy did not even consider attending college. He did not want to later regret not attempting to play professionally.

So, Andy became a professional tennis player before his high school graduation in 2000. That spring, he joined the **ATP** Tour. But he continued competing on its junior circuit.

Andy was ranked number one internationally on the junior circuit in summer 2000. And later that year, he won a junior boys' title at the U.S. Open!

To gain more experience, Andy also played on the challenger circuit. This circuit is considered the minor league of professional tennis. Nearly every ATP player has gained recognition and talent by competing in challenger games.

Andy closed the 2000 season as the number one junior in the world. He was the first American in eight years to achieve this honor.

Magazines and newspapers made Andy a household name. It wasn't long before eager fans wanted Andy's autograph.

Andy continued to impress on the courts in 2001. In February, he made his first Davis Cup appearance. The Davis Cup is an annual men's international team tennis event. That year, France claimed victory.

In April, Andy won the Verizon Tennis Challenge. This was his first professional men's singles title. A week later, he earned his second professional title at the U.S. Men's Clay Court Championships.

The young star also gained international attention at the 2001 French Open. There, Andy defeated Michael Chang in an exhausting five-**set** battle. Unfortunately, Andy was eliminated in the third round. However, he finished 2001 as the youngest player in the **ATP** Top 20.

Andy continues to exhibit good sportsmanship as he congratulates Chang on a game well played at the 2001 French Open.

U.S. Open Champion

In 2002, Roddick played in all four Grand Slam events. He performed his best at the U.S. Open. There, he reached the quarterfinals.

By August 2002, Roddick was ranked number nine on the **ATP** Tour. And by early September, he had earned more than $1.65 million in prize money from his professional career. Roddick ended the year as the youngest American in the ATP Top Ten since 1992!

However, Roddick felt he needed a change. So after losing in the first round of the 2003 French Open, he decided to switch coaches. In June, Roddick began working with Brad Gilbert. Gilbert had coached tennis star Andre Agassi to six Grand Slam titles between 1994 and 2002.

Coach Gilbert and Roddick

Over time, Gilbert helped Roddick improve his skills. Together, they focused on footwork, **backhands**, net game, and returns. They also worked on conditioning, as well as Roddick's mental game. Gilbert encouraged Roddick not to dwell on his mistakes. Instead, he told him to focus on beating the opponent.

After less than a month of working with Gilbert, Roddick made it to the Wimbledon semifinals. Two months later, he won the U.S. Open!

Roddick won his first professional Grand Slam title at the 2003 U.S. Open. He finished the season as the number one singles player in the world!

On Tour

Roddick continued to claim wins in 2004. His victories led him to his first Wimbledon title match in July. There, he suffered a heartbreaking loss to Swiss tennis powerhouse Roger Federer.

2004 U.S. Davis Cup team: (*from left*) Captain Patrick McEnroe, Mike Bryan, Bob Bryan, Andy Roddick, and Mardy Fish

In August, Roddick represented the United States in the Summer Olympics in Athens, Greece. However, he lost in the third round to Chile's Fernando Gonzalez.

In addition to the **ATP** Tour, Roddick continued to play on the U.S. Davis Cup team. He helped lead his team to its first final since 1997. In December, the United States played in the final against Spain. But Spain defeated the United States 3–2.

By the end of 2004, Roddick had captured a career-high 74 match wins on the ATP circuit. He became the first

American to win 70 or more matches in back-to-back seasons since Pete Sampras.

Following the Davis Cup final, Roddick and his teammates hit the road. They wanted to promote tennis throughout America. So, they played **exhibition** matches in cities that the men's professional tour does not visit.

During their road trip, Roddick, Fish, and the Bryan twins made unscheduled stops and held tennis clinics in various cities.

At the end of 2005, Roddick was ranked the number one American on the ATP Tour.

Roddick's 2005 season mirrored 2004. In July, he played in the Wimbledon finals. Yet again, he lost to Federer. Then in August, Roddick played in the U.S. Open. However, he was defeated in the first round after three tiebreakers.

In September, Roddick participated in the Davis Cup World Group **play-offs**. There, he helped his team slug out a five-**set** win against Belgium. This 4-hour, 32-minute match was the longest U.S. Davis Cup game since tiebreakers were introduced in 1989!

In January 2006, Roddick played in the Australian Open, but lost in the fourth round. Then in May, he retired in the first round of the French Open because of an ankle injury. Roddick's ankle healed enough for him to compete in the Wimbledon tournament in July. But unfortunately, he was defeated in the third round.

Opposite Page: The 2005 U.S. Davis Cup team members posed together before their match against Belgium. Members are (*from left*) Andy Roddick, Bob Bryan, Captain Patrick McEnroe, Mike Bryan, and James Blake.

25

Roddick Today

Andy Roddick remains the public face of American tennis. Off the court, he enjoys spending time with his friends, watching movies, and listening to music. He especially likes boating, waterskiing, and skydiving. Roddick is also a loyal University of Nebraska sports fan.

In 2001, Roddick started the Andy Roddick Foundation. It focuses on keeping children healthy and educated. Roddick's mother directs the effort. The foundation often holds events to raise money for its causes. In 2005, the organization raised more than $800,000 at an event in Austin.

Roddick is a regular at other charity events, too. In 2005, he participated in the Serving for Tsunami Relief tennis **exhibition**. This event raised more than $500,000 for victims in Asia.

Despite his growing success, Roddick remains humble. His heroes include bicyclist Lance Armstrong, as well as his **mentor** and fellow tennis professional Andre Agassi. Roddick admires how both men have fought hard to make incredible comebacks.

Roddick also retains a sense of patriotism. He is proud to play on the U.S. Davis Cup team. And in the future, he hopes to play at another Olympics. "Getting asked to represent your country is, I think, the highest honor one can get in sports," Roddick said.

Roddick helps raise money for the Kids Tennis Foundation. This organization aims to give disadvantaged Australian children the opportunity to play tennis.

Glossary

Association for Tennis Professionals (ATP) - a professional men's tennis circuit that regulates tournaments around the world.

backhand - a tennis stroke made with the back of the hand turned outward and the arm drawn across the body.

charisma (kuh-RIHZ-muh) - a special magnetic charm or appeal.

doubles - a tennis competition featuring two players on each side of the net.

exhibition - a public showing of athletic skill.

forehand - a tennis stroke made with the palm of the hand turned forward and the arm held outward from the body.

intense - marked by great energy, determination, or concentration.

mentor - a guide who serves as a good example.

passionate - capable of expressing strong feeling.

play-off - a series of games played after the end of a regular sports season to determine which teams will compete in a championship.

scholarship - a gift of money to help a student pay for instruction.

set - a group of six or more games that make up a unit of a tennis match.

Web Sites

To learn more about Andy Roddick, visit ABDO Publishing Company on the World Wide Web at **www.abdopublishing.com**. Web sites about Roddick are featured on our Book Links page. These links are routinely monitored and updated to provide the most current information available.

Index

A
Agassi, Andre 20, 26
Andy Roddick
      Foundation 26
Armstrong, Lance 26

B
Becker, Boris 6
Belgium 24
Benhabiles, Tarik 10,
      12

C
Chang, Michael 18
Chile 22

D
Davis Cup 18, 22,
      23, 24, 27

E
Eddie Herr
      International
      Junior
      Tournament 12
education 10, 12, 16

F
family 6, 7, 8, 12, 16,
      26
Federer, Roger 22, 24
Fish, Mardy 12
France 10, 18

G
Gilbert, Brad 20, 21
Gonzalez, Fernando
      22
Grand Slam events
      12, 16, 18, 20, 21,
      22, 24
Greece 22

H
hobbies 10, 26

L
Lendl, Ivan 6

M
McEnroe, John 5
McEnroe, Patrick 4

O
Olympics 22, 27

R
Reebok 8

S
Sampras, Pete 23
Spain 22
Switzerland 22

U
U.S. Men's Clay Court
      Championships 18

V
Verizon Tennis
      Challenge 18